D0575994

JAN 0 4 01

WILD CATS

Pumas

Anne Welsbacher
ABDO Publishing Company

THIS BOOK IS THE PROPERTY
THE NATIONAL CITY PUBLIC LIBRARY
CHILDREN'S ROOM

visit us at
www.abdopub.com

Published by Abdo Publishing Company 4940 Viking Drive, Edina, Minnesota 55435. Copyright © 2000 by Abdo Consulting Group, Inc. International copyrights reserved in all countries. No part of this book may be reproduced in any form without written permission from the publisher.

Printed in the United States.

Photo credits: Peter Arnold, Inc.

Edited by Lori Kinstad Pupeza
Contributing editor Morgan Hughes

Library of Congress Cataloging-in-Publication Data

Welsbacher, Anne, 1955-
      Pumas / Anne Welsbacher.
      p. cm. -- (Wild cats)
      Includes index.
      Summary: Describes the physical characteristics, behaviors, and habitats of this wild cat found in many places throughout the world.
      ISBN 1-57765-091-3
      1. Pumas--Juvenile literature. [1. Pumas.] I. Title. II. Series: Welsbacher, Anne, 1955- Wild cats.
      QL737.C23W4475   2000
      599.75'24--dc21

                                            98-16644
                                          CIP
                                          AC

Contents

Wild Cats around the World

The puma is one kind of wild cat. Pumas live in the western United States, Mexico, Central America, and South America. Other wild cats live in Africa, Asia, India, and the Middle East.

Pumas have brown or tan fur, about the same color as the fur of a lion. Pumas are sometimes called mountain lions. But pumas are different from mountain lions.

The puma has other names, too. It is called cougar, catamount, panther, or painter. It is even called mountain screamer because of the screaming sounds the female puma sometimes makes.

Pumas are good jumpers. They like to sit in high places.

Pumas also are good at climbing and **stalking**. Pumas can swim, too. But like most cats, wild or tame, they do not like the water!

Pumas are sometimes called mountain lions.

Big Cat, Little Cat

*M*ost wild cats are much bigger than house cats. But they are like house cats in many ways.

Both big cats and little cats have whiskers. They use them like fingers, to feel their way along small spaces. And all cats can see at night, better than people can!

Most big and little cats can pull their sharp claws into their soft paws. They stretch them out to scratch or climb, and pull them in to run or rest.

Pumas like to be by themselves even more than most cats. When they see a person, they disappear behind bushes or rocks. They hunt and live alone.

Pumas are like house cats in one special way. They purr like house cats. They do not roar like many wild cats.

Big cats and little cats are very graceful. They can balance in high places, and jump and land without knocking things over. Pumas are one of the most graceful of all cats.

Pumas use their whiskers to feel their way along small spaces.

A Closer Look

*P*umas have tan, golden, or reddish-brown coats. A little gray at the very tip of each hair makes the fur seem to shine in the sunlight. Pumas have white fur on their bellies, necks, and chests.

The puma is the largest cat that lives in the United States. They are not in the same class as the big cats, like lions, tigers, or cheetahs. But a puma is still longer than a person is tall!

Pumas have great big paws. They have long, thick tails. The tail helps the puma balance on branches or on high mountain cliffs.

A puma has big paws, a thick tail, and white fur on its belly, neck, and chest.

The Puma at Home

Pumas can **adapt** to different places. This means that pumas are able to learn how to survive in different parts of the world.

Pumas live in jungles, mountains, grasslands, and deserts. In the United States, many live in the Rocky Mountains or the hot desert areas of the Southwest.

Pumas need water to drink, food to eat, and places where they can climb trees or hide. The area and climate a puma lives in is called its **habitat**.

Pumas like high places. They like to sit on cliffs or mountains high above valleys or grasslands. They watch the world from their perch. They hide or rest behind rocks, under bushes, or in trees.

Pumas live in a wide variety of habitats.

A Champion Jumper

Pumas are amazing jumpers. They are very **agile**. The puma's long tail helps it balance when it jumps. Its long legs help it jump high and far.

Pumas can jump right into high trees in one bound! They can jump 12 feet (4 m) high from a standing point. That is like jumping onto the roof of a porch or shed!

Pumas can also jump forward long distances. If you take 10 to 15 big steps forward, that is how far a puma can jump in a single leap!

Pumas can hear and see very well. They can see along the horizon and on each side. They can see things far away or almost behind them.

Pumas almost never attack people. Chances are you will never see a puma, even if you are in a place where pumas live. That is because the puma sees you first, and slips away into a **secret** hiding place.

Pumas are great jumpers.

13

The Predator's Prey

Pumas are **carnivores**. They also are called **predators**. The animals they eat are called **prey**.

Pumas eat big animals like deer, elk, and bighorn sheep. They eat small, quick animals like rabbits, ducks, chipmunks, squirrels, birds, beavers, and mice.

Pumas eat what they can find. This is another way that pumas **adapt**, or change when needed, to survive.

The puma hunts by **stalking** an animal. It springs forward and knocks down the animal. It twists the animal's neck with its strong, big paws until the neck breaks.

Then the puma carries its kill to a hiding place. It eats as much as it can. Then it buries the animal to hide it.

The puma returns every one or two days until it has eaten every bit of the animal. The puma's rough tongue even scrapes meat off the bones. Sometimes it can take up to two weeks for a puma to finish eating an animal.

A puma with prey in its mouth.

Cat to Cat

Pumas do not like to be near other pumas or animals. Each puma has its own **territory**.

Males do not invade the territories of other males. But sometimes females live in parts of the territories of other pumas.

Territories change with seasons. Pumas follow their **prey** as they **migrate** from cold places to warmer places.

Pumas do not roar, but they make other interesting sounds. When a female wants to **mate**, she makes a high screaming sound. When a mother calls her young, she makes a chirping meow. When young pumas cry for their mother, they make a screeching whistle sound. And pumas purr, too, just like a pet cat!

A puma's territory changes with the seasons.

17

Cat Families

*I*n cold northern places, pumas have babies, called cubs or kittens, in the early spring. Then the kittens can grow in the warm months of summer. In warmer places, pumas have kittens any time of year.

The female puma raises her cubs alone. She makes a safe home under a ledge or near a group of rocks. She can give birth to as many as six cubs, but most of the time she has two or three cubs.

The cubs are born with spots. Later, the spots will disappear. Their eyes are closed and they cannot walk.

A few hours after they are born, they **nurse** their mother. In only a few weeks, they will start to eat meat. But they keep nursing, too, until they are three months or even older. This is longer than most **predators**.

A puma mother with cubs in her den.

Growing Up

*T*he mother must leave her kittens to go hunting. They stay quietly in their hidden home until she returns with food for them and herself.

But soon the cubs begin to learn what they must know as adult pumas. They grow fast. By the time they are about two weeks old, they begin to explore.

They practice hunting. They **stalk** grasshoppers and blowing grass. They practice on their mother! They bite her ears, swat her tail, and climb all over her.

By the time the cubs are eight weeks old, they join their mother on her hunting trips. They share their food without fighting each other.

When the young pumas are one to almost two years old, they are ready to be on their own. Sometimes their mother leaves and finds another place to live. Other times, the cubs leave to find their own homes.

A young puma might take three or four years to find its new home. Or it might find a place to live right away, not too far—but not too close—to the place where it grew up.

A puma mother cleans her cub.

Glossary

Agile—able to jump and balance easily.

Adapt—to change when needed; for example, if it is summer, a puma eats animals that live in hot weather, but if it is winter, a puma can catch and eat animals that live in cold weather, too.

Carnivore—an animal that eats meat.

Habitat—the area and climate that an animal lives in.

Mate—to join in a pair in order to produce young.

Migrate—to move from one region to another with the change of seasons, or in search of food.

Nurse—baby pumas getting milk from their mother.

Predator—an animal that eats other animals.

Prey—an animal that is eaten by other animals.

Secretive—hidden and alone, staying away from others.

Stalk—to sneak up on something.

Territory—an area or place where certain animals live; if others enter this area, the animal might fight or scare them off.

Internet Sites

Tiger Information Center
http://www.5tigers.org/
The Tiger Information Center is dedicated to providing information to help preserve the remaining five subspecies of tigers. This is a great site, with many links, sound, and animation.

The Lion Research Center
http://www.lionresearch.org/
Everything you want to know about lions is here. Lion research and conservation in Africa, information on lion behavior, and updates from researchers in the Serengeti about specific lion prides.

The Cheetah Spot
http://ThingsWild.com/cheetah2.html
This is a cool spot with sound and animation. Lots of fun information.

Amur Leopard
http://www.scz.org/asian/amurl1.html
This site links you to some great zoo spots. Very informative.

These sites are subject to change. Go to your favorite search engine and type in "cats" for more sites.

PASS IT ON
Tell Others What You Like About Animals!

To educate readers around the country, pass on interesting tips about animals, maybe a fun story about your animal or pet, and little-known facts about animals. We want to hear from you!

To get posted on the ABDO Publishing Company Web site, email us at "animals@abdopub.com"
Visit us at www.abdopub.com

Index